My Favorite Reflections is a compilation of editorials that have appeared in the *Brethren Missionary Herald* magazine. You will find a theme running through the book. The theme centers on the thought of the world created by God; a world filled to overflowing with exciting, though seemingly small, events. In these everyday happenings we should be able to find a moral or practical lesson that can be applied with benefit to our Christian lives. We so often complain of living in dull and uninteresting circumstances. Life is not dull, it is made up of days the Lord has made. To those who will search, an exciting world of small things with big truths can be found.

Join me in a walk through this world, your world, and see in your family, your occupation, and your environment those lessons accompanied by strange delights. You may have seen them before, but now let's review them and relate to their meaning.

— C.W.T.

My Favorite Reflections

Charles W. Turner

BMH BOOKS
Winona Lake, Indiana 46590

Dedicated to a man
*who is more than a memory,
a man of God who taught
me by word and example, who
served God humbly and with sincerity.
A man who is with His God
and to whom I owe so very much . . .*
my father, Charles H. Turner.

COVER PHOTO: Washington's Mount Rainier and Reflection Lake.
(Photo by Ed Cooper of H. Armstrong Roberts)

ISBN: 0-88469-029-6

COPYRIGHT 1976
BMH BOOKS
WINONA LAKE, INDIANA

Printed in U.S.A.

Acknowledgments

To friends who have taught me to see grace and love in flesh.

To Tim Kennedy for the art work and cover design.

To the readers of the *Herald* magazine who have encouraged me by their kind comments through the years.

To Fern Sandy for being a friend as well as an editorial secretary, and to Ken Herman for helpful suggestions and work in layout.

Table of Contents

A Turtle on the Turnpike 9
"She was lonely ... so she got a cat" 13
Now They Are Slowing Down My Catsup! 17
"Lord, why do I always get in the wrong line?" 21
Adjusting to the Unusual Is One Thing,
    But Earthquakes Scare Me................. 25
Even Robins Make Mistakes 29
"Happy Birthday, Dad" or My First New Bicycle 33
My Willie Can Do It! 37
A Government School for Coyotes *(The sheep are
    being attacked again)* 41
I'm OK, You're OK, But He's Perfect 45
Whatever Happened to $1.98 Sneakers? 49
Analysis Paralysis 53
A Nickel Tip and Gospel Tract 57
Rumble Seats, Running Boards, and Patriotism....... 61
A Stone, Some Paint, and Thanks................. 65
You Can't Hit a Home Run Every Time 69
A Progressive Alternative to Busing................ 73

A
Turtle on the Turnpike

Few experiences in life can be as frustrating as finding oneself in a place where he or she should not be. What do you do at a time like that? For the one with great foresight the answer is simple—don't go there in the first place. You and I cannot argue with such wisdom. Nevertheless, sometimes unplanned circumstances do evolve into frustrating situations. Recently, I saw a very dramatic demonstration of this truth!

It was early in the morning, and I was driving along the Pennsylvania Turnpike. Up ahead I noticed an object in the road, and as I drove nearer it became more obvious as to what the object was . . . a turtle! It was resting in the center of the right-hand lane of traffic. He had retracted into his shell—pulling in his four legs and tail. The only sign of life was his head which was out far enough to size up the problem. Would you accept my reasoning that he must have been in the process of analyzing the total situation before proceeding one more step? Let me assure you the dilemma had no easy answer. To proceed would mean crossing one more lane of traffic, plus a median strip, and two more lanes of traffic before he could be safe again. To turn back may have appeared to be the next best solution. Never having had the faculty of thinking "turtle thoughts," I don't know what his logic could have been. There may have been one real good way out for him if a "Good Samaritan" would have been around to stop and pick up the poor fellow and thus remove him to safety.

Even that device could have presented problems. Number one, the big road signs said, "Emergency Parking Only." Would the state trooper judge this as an emergency? Number two, who knows but what the turtle may have been a determined creature who had some important business on the other side of the turnpike. Such "help" would really have been a hindrance to his dedicated mission! Sorry, I cannot give you the final chapter of the turtle's tour of the turnpike. (I wasn't the "Good Samaritan.") However, please bear with me while I record for you some of the mental observations I had for the next few miles of my trip.

Having spent more or less all of my adult life working with people, I can remember a lot of human beings who were like the turtle. In fact, I can recall a number of occasions when I was just like him. There are those times in life when we all find ourselves in unusual circumstances and places, and we wonder how we ever managed to arrive at such a state of affairs. Yes, some strenuous thinking might help to answer the question for us. However, it undoubtedly took an untold number of turns and decisions to bring us to the present predicament. The "now" was where we found ourselves, and that was not where we wanted to be. The traffic was buzzing around us, and it seemed any move might be fatal. But to remain in the present place created an equal number of hazards.

Perhaps our first thought was . . . how do we get out of here? Shall we keep on going or turn back? That is the pressing question. Maybe our purpose in getting involved was a good one and not of bad intent. To go on may take more courage than it seems possible to muster at the moment. To turn back might well mean a personal defeat in our lives. Decisions are not always easy to come by, and we need help.

But where is the help coming from? You guessed it— from the friend who shrewdly reminds you that you should not have let yourself get into this situation. (Big help!) Then there is always the possibility that someone will stop and give you the real assistance that is needed to solve the problem. He might want to remove you from danger and place you in safety, but remember—in order to complete the task and reach safety, you may have to retrace those slow, painful steps.

Going through danger is not foreign to the servants of the Lord. The Bible is filled with such types of commissions from God. David, Daniel and Jeremiah are a few of God's saints who were led in paths of severe trial. The main idea here is to make certain God told you to "cross the road."

As the turtle's image faded in my mind, I was torn between several thoughts. After all, it was just a turtle . . . but, "Lord, never let me become insensitive to the needs of others. Never let me as a believer become thoughtless, cold or hardened to the dilemmas of others. Don't let me lose my love . . . this is serious. Give me wisdom to know when and how to help someone. Please, do not let me make them retrace their steps when You want them to go forward."

"She was lonely...

so she got a cat!"

The above simple headline was dated November 16, 1975, Chicago. It caught my attention on a Sunday morning just before I left my home for a church service. What was described as the "biggest cat roundup in the history of the dog pound" resulted in the hauling away of 96 cats via three trucks. Later this record was disputed because about three months previous 146 cats had been removed from a "South Side" home in Chicago.

A lady who was called Ruth had lived alone in her home for the past eight years since her mother's death. Ruth, 54 years old, was reported by a neighbor to have been lonely since the passing of her mother, and four years ago acquired her first cat, and then another, and another, and on and on. When the animal-control crew entered the house, they found wall-to-wall cats in the bedroom, living room, and even in the kitchen refrigerator.

My first reaction to the story was one of light humor. My imagination ran away with me as I envisioned what happened when the house door was opened and the cats came forth! Not being particularly fond of cats, I also entertained some negative thoughts about living with a hundred cats—give or take a few. With the price of cat food at the present level, it would be an expensive luxury to maintain such a feline gathering!

But there was also a very sad note in the whole story, and it was Ruth. The headlines said a lot, "She was lonely . . . so she got a cat." The question occurred to me— "How many 'Ruths' are there in this world of ours?" More than we would ever imagine possible. Every community has a number of Ruths whom we all pass by each day without so much as a wave or a nod or even a little smile and a "hello." I have noticed so many people who want to talk to someone. They are lonely and tired and feel neglected in a world that does not seem to want or need them. Everyone is in such a hurry that there is not a person who will stop and listen to a few words because those words do not seem to be important. But communication is important to the "Ruths" of this world.

Recently I spoke at a dinner meeting sponsored by a Christian women's organization. After it was all over, a little "Ruth" caught me and told me what she had done during the previous four days. Not one of the events was earthshaking or even very exciting to me. They were in fact quite dull and ordinary, and she forgot several times in the conversation where she had been. Although others waited to speak to me, I decided to give this little lady her fair share of time. She wanted to share a part of her life with someone else, and I happened to be the chosen one at the time. How important events are in a person's own life, even though they may seem inconsequential to others. And let's be fair, if something cannot be shared, it loses most of its true value.

I personally find a sense of guilt when I rush through a conversation with an obviously lonely person. I am reminded of another incident one time following a message in a church service when a person "got hold" of me, and it seemed the conversation would never end. I was far from home and there was a great deal of business to transact and people were waiting. Believe it or not, I remained "to listen." Some weeks later a letter came across the country to me after I had returned home. It contained a Thank You note from the person for the time we had spent in con-

My Favorite Reflections • 15

versation. I am glad I had not been too busy that day to stand and share. I shared my "ear" with a lonely heart who was looking for a friend.

Have we as Christians become too busy with our church meetings and organizations? Are we so busy we do not have time to share ourselves with the "Ruths" of this world? How about the person who is lonely and needs a friend just to listen for a few minutes to the "big" event that happened last week. You may not be thrilled with the news, but you will be rewarded to know you helped make someone's day for them.

Do not make your "Ruth" gather a hundred cats because there is no human being with whom she can communicate and share.

Now
They
Are
Slowing
Down
My
Catsup!

My Favorite Reflections • 17

At times I feel the whole world is conspiring against me. This is not merely a complex of thinking the world has singled me out as its number one victim, though this may be involved. By nature and temperament I am basically an impatient person. I detest long lines at checkouts, and patient waiting is not my best trait! It seems I have an impatient streak that runs from the top of my head to the soles of my feet. I am not particularly proud of this, and I am working on it.

My wife has been pointing to those articles in the *Reader's Digest* about heart attacks and personality traits. Everyone, the doctor says, is either an "A," "B," or "C" person. The "A's" naturally have a monopoly on heart attacks; those in the "B" class have a few attacks, but nothing to get excited about. The "C's," I am quick to tell her, would not know whether or not they had an attack because they don't get excited about much of anything. (Well, maybe their blood pressure will mount just a little if there is a late welfare check!) Mrs. Turner is using all this "important" data to tell me to slow it down a bit. However, I interpret all this "A," "B," "C" material as an attack on the free enterprise system. But she says no—it is all reliable and trustworthy (and I should profit by it), because the *Reader's Digest*, next to the Bible, is the most dependable literature in the world!

Now, please listen. Out of the six o'clock news the other evening came a commercial obviously written by a "C" personality. It told how slow the catsup comes from a bottle of Heinz. I thought it was a joke at first, but after viewing it for several nights I concluded it is all serious. My reaction was to tell the grocery shopper in our house never to buy another bottle of the *slow-pouring catsup*. I just do not have time for such luxury. Have we really come to the place where all we have to do is gaze up in the nozzle of a catsup bottle and wait for the results to pour out on our hot dog that is rapidly cooling in the transaction. My patience was tried just thinking of this agonizing ordeal.

Certainly I know it is a small thing to wait for 20 seconds for a drip of catsup. But this is just my way of saying that we human beings spend our time in very strange ways! There are some Christians who waste their time in ways as peculiar as the "catsup-watchers." Valuable time is spent in endless bickering and useless discussion. Time is spent in unprofitable analysis of unimportant topics. Paul spoke of discussions that were endless in nature and that never brought any constructive conclusions or results.

We as Christians have available more power but seem to use less "go" than any other known group. The dynamite of the gospel of Jesus Christ is literally set to blow this old world apart. It has been placed in our trust—in our hands and in our lives—and yet it remains unused. Some churches have been on the same corner with the same sign out front for years and have made almost no impact on their community. It is not the lack of availability of God's power that creates the stagnation. It is the lack of permission by Christians to be used that finds God thwarted in working on an individual level.

It is about time we become aware of our opportunities for service and begin to get a little excited about the power of God. What are we waiting for or what are we hoping for that will get us motivated? Maybe you are fascinated in the wait for the slow-moving catsup to fall and have allotted plenty of time for the wait. I would much prefer to have the catsup pour quickly so I could get back to doing something more constructive.

It looks to me like we need some more "A" type Christians and a lot less of the "C" type. There certainly is a risk in activity, and this includes Christian activity, but the risk is small in relationship to the rewards which are great. The time is growing later than we think! When the end comes, I trust we will be found *serving* and *doing* for God rather than spending our time with minor things.

"Lord, why do I always get in the wrong line?"

My Favorite Reflections • 21

Several months ago I was in my usual state of rush when I discovered it was necessary to purchase some postage stamps. Upon entering the post office, I noticed four lines waiting at the windows. There were long lines at all but one of the windows, therefore, with great haste and joy I joined the shortest line. I was in a hurry and wanted to save a few minutes of my precious time, and be on my way. My joy was a very short lived one because the young lady ahead of me opened a shopping bag and from it she took about fifteen small packages! Each one of them had to be weighed and insured and placed in the proper mail bag. The lines to the right of me moved with great speed; the line to the left of me moved even faster. Yes, I did what every other impatient person would do, I switched lines and waited for my stamps. Then what did I see? Yes, you guessed correctly—the line I had left began to move and the one I was in . . . came to a dead stop.

Have you ever switched lanes of traffic only to find you had inadvertently chosen the slow moving one? Or, have you ever had the feeling while in a line at McDonalds that your clerk was the slowest in the business? It does happen, and when it happens I often say: "Lord, why do I always get in the wrong line?" I have never yet had a direct answer to the question, but I do have some rather strong thoughts on what the answer might be.

Let me share with you some of the reflections on the subject. I am (and perhaps you are, too) one of the by-products of a generation in a hurry. Speed—speed is what counts. Now, what we are all hurrying to do may be in question, but nevertheless we are in a hurry. For instance, I have never been able to figure out why when I get on an

Interstate Highway and I know there is not a stop light for three thousand miles—yet the traffic is only moving at a snail's pace. It just doesn't make sense to me. So I impatiently wait, while in my heart I am moving. We have been instilled with the philosophy that all things must move—and NOW. Though there is some merit in this argument, there are also fallacies. Everything does not move at our direction and dictation.

Another thought concerning this matter of waiting is that it points out our own self-esteem. We want everything to move when we want it to move so it will be convenient for us. If the line is short—I do not have to wait. The stress is on the I. So much of our impatience stems from the problem of our personal desires and plans being thwarted.

When standing in the slow line I find my conscious thoughts dwelling on the possibility that God wants to talk to me. It may be He is suggesting that I should slow down a little. As I read the writings of David and Isaiah I am impressed with the emphasis on waiting and the need for patience. These distinctives are little practiced in the age in which we live. There are many, many things we miss by moving so rapidly.

One of the blessings of the 55 mile-an-hour limit for me is that I see more scenery along the way. When you drove a car at the speeds formerly allowed it was necessary to be alert to what was in front of you. Too much gazing at the landscape was a pastime which had to be forfeited. Now I am discovering anew the beauty of our wooded hills and valleys, the nostalgia of an old farmhouse and the barn lot. Along the way I see that some trees are pines, some are maples, others are oaks, and they are no longer only blurs of green standing on wooden stems.

This slower pace opens the way for spiritual benefits as well. We try to read seven chapters in the Bible in seven minutes. However, God never intended us to use "speed reading" for spiritual growth. We hurry because we do not think we have enough time. Time for what? How do we determine our priorities? The premium of a long line may be greater time to learn to patiently wait on God. Or it might be a time to think upon all of the good things which He has given to us as believers.

The next time you get in the slow line at the checkout counter of the supermarket, use the waiting time to some profit and good. Taking your impatience out on the poor clerk is not the answer. Remember, many of the clerks are merely products of modern education, and the new math takes time to figure out what 2 plus 2 really is. So smile and talk to God. Think how great it is to be a Christian! It certainly beats line switching—believe me!!

Adjusting to the Unusual Is One Thing, But Earthquakes Scare Me

Indiana is a cold, cold place during the month of January. On further thought . . . December, February and March are not times when you will enjoy too many heat waves, either. The thought of a business trip to Southern California, in the midst of winter, was not the worst thing I could contemplate in the line of duty. So, I packed up ready for a respite from the freezing breezes and blowing snow.

My wishes were not in vain because when I arrived in sunny California, I found the climate much to my liking. Somehow the whole world looked a bit brighter. The smog was nil and the sun shone in warm, satisfying abundance. Why did I ever have a bad thought about California? (My conscience bothered me a little bit!) Everything went well . . . with a good conference and seminar, a great time of fellowship, and a time of exchange of ideas with others in the publishing world. What more could a man ask in the cold, cold month of January?

My thoughts were soon to receive quite a jar. It was three o'clock in the early morning hours and all was well. I was sleeping on the eighth floor of the Holiday Inn in Long Beach, when suddenly I was aroused. The glass sliding doors were sliding and my bed was moving. Yes; indeed, an earth tremor in the area was making things feel different than normal. My first impulse was to run to the dresser and check my flight insurance. I was curious to see if I was covered if I took flight from that particular area! However, before I could concentrate on any other rational thought, it was all quiet once more.

The next evening as I sat talking to a friend it happened again! This time it was two minutes before midnight. What a way to close a day! In talking to the native Californians, during the next couple of days, I found they were impressed, but not overly awed by the happenings. You see, what was so unusual to me was not strange to them. They rather acted and talked as if earthquakes served a purpose, like stirring their coffee in the morning or shaking the oranges out of the trees. As I started to reflect on the whole matter, I thought there must be an editorial in this whole phenomenon . . . and sure enough I found it. Let's call it "Adjusting to the Unusual."

The act of adjusting can be good or it can be bad. My first reaction to the quaking earth was negative because I thought it would take a few trial and error experiences for me to calmly accept such episodes. I just didn't feel that earth tremors and yours truly were too compatible. This line of thinking leads me to the conclusion that it is possible to be around something negative for a period of time and eventually become adjusted to its presence. Sin is a great deal like that. I know some matters in question may be classified as wrong and yet a constant exposure causes one to finally let down his guard, and soon he just blinks his eye and goes on his way. This can happen in any number of circumstances—we *abhor* . . . then we *tolerate* . . . then we *succumb* to the evil.

Our life in a busy secular world is by necessity complicated. We are confronted with principles and actions that are contrary to the teachings of the Bible. Remember, we are not removed from the presence of sin when we are saved. It ever remains to confront us, but in the name of Jesus Christ, we can gain the victory. It is a known fact that our attitude toward sin is determined by our relationship with the Son of God.

Yet, there are unusual truths that we need to adjust to and accept. The natural man finds Biblical truth unnatural to him because it is supernatural. Through the new birth and salvation a person moves into a new life pattern. This pattern can be a dramatic change of purpose and intention as God directs. To move fully into this Christ-directed life is an existing and challenging spiritual adjustment.

So, adjusting to the unusual is good IF it means moving from the domination of sin to the freedom in the Son. It is bad when it means the good is encompassed about with evil, and if we accept and adjust to the wrong situation.

Remembering that from little tremors mighty earthquakes do grow, I left beautiful California the next day with mixed emotions. Sunny California was exchanged for a cold, windy Indiana night with a temperature of about ten degrees above zero. Oh, well, it does take a little time to adjust, you know.

Even Robins Make Mistakes

March has been very unusual in Indiana this year. It was beautiful; a great deal of sunshine and none of those nasty, late winter storms. But it happened! We awoke to a winter fairyland of wet snow covering the entire landscape. From inside the nice warm house the outside scenery was beautiful to behold. However, the picture was not quite the same when you got behind the wheel of an automobile and tried to move through what the storm had dumped.

Unfortunately, one can only spend so long at home, and then out into weather you must go. There I met her—the first robin of spring (?). She had found one of the few bare spots right in the middle of the road. Not being a mind reader or too conversant with robins, I nevertheless detected a reluctance upon her part to yield the right-of-way. She sat as long as possible and then took flight. She seemed to possess the attitude of having one of those bad days that we all experience, when cooperation is not what we have in mind. She seemed to be saying: "OK—I made a mistake by being here. I left Florida too soon, but the least you could do is not to add to my misery." At least that is what I think she would have said, that is if she said something. Even robins make mistakes and their timing is bad.

We have all experienced bad timing. Remember the time you met a friend and tried to be funny, only to find out that he had just gone through a difficult experience. Or have you been invited out to dinner and, through error, arrived an hour earlier than the hostess expected you? Perhaps it happened the other way, and you got there an hour late and everyone was patiently (?) waiting. Time and timing are very important; and it is possible to be wrong regarding them in two ways—ahead of time, behind time

... early or late, either will cause problems.

God is always perfect in His timing. The Bible tells us that "when the fulness of time was come, God sent forth his son." It was perfect timing for all the factors of human need, and God's plan had reached that point in history when it was time to act. He did. Jesus Christ came to this world to bring salvation and through it—hope. The world was not ready to receive Christ, but the opportunity to do so was given.

There is a lesson to be learned for us who serve the Lord. We need to be as careful as possible to work on God's time schedule and not our own. We become overly anxious at times to see the work of Christ go forward. It is at this point that we put too much of self-effort into the task and too little of the power of the Spirit of God. This is running before the Lord and will not bear the lasting fruit we desire to see. It is also possible to be careless and indifferent toward God which will cause us to reject His leading and timing. When this takes place we become prone to put off the work until it is too late. Opportunities then can pass us by and possibly never return.

So, it is not only important *what* we do but *when* we do it. Does the task seem too difficult and the way too hard? Take another look, and keep in mind that it is God's work and He desires to see it accomplished. It takes wisdom and God promises wisdom to those who will ask. It would appear that proper timing in the Christian life really comes down to the fact that it is Holy Spirit leadership that we are talking about. God will supply this if and when we really want it.

My robin friend appeared to be a little too early, but a

few days later the bright sunshine of spring returned, and I feel she ought to be happy now.

Patience, praying, waiting and being willing to move by His guidance will bring joy to the Christian who is laboring for God and waiting on His time.

"Happy Birthday, Dad"

or

My First New Bicycle

My Favorite Reflections • 33

Some things in life are best enjoyed if you wait a long time for them. So it was with great joy that this year's birthday brought a long-awaited prize—a new bike. My only other bicycle came to me early in life. It was a used one, and the chain slipped from the day it was purchased until it finally refused to go anymore. Nevertheless, it was some basic transportation for a few years. But my new one is something else. It is English made, ten-speed, with hand brakes, and has all the things that are supposed to be up to date. With it came the surprise greetings: "Happy Birthday, Dad."

What good is a new bike if you can't use it? So on the first day of possession I took off with my son, Jeff, and his buddy, Duane, for a ride on our bicycles. The temperature was thirty degrees because it was January in Indiana. The wind was blowing about twenty miles an hour and it was cold! We started out for the nearest town which was only eight miles away. (Since I had not ridden a bike for about thirty years, I didn't want to go too far!) With the wind to our backs and us full of energy, the problems were small. A few dogs chased us from their quiet rural homes, but we whizzed along with all ten-speeds working in perfect order. After a bit of refreshment, we started home. The dogs began to look bigger, in fact, a yellow cat walked out of a farm lot and she looked threatening to me. The wind was blowing in my face, and I had to pedal to get down the hills, and the ten-speeds stuck, and now I had only one left. For some reason my legs got tired of pumping. To put it briefly; at the end of the line I was convinced this was about the longest sixteen miles I had ever put in. Since the bike was so tired when I got home I have let it rest in the garage for the past two weeks.

Bike riding is a great deal like the Christian experience I soon learned. Much of the time you have to ride into the wind and that is never easy. It is so much more pleasant to have the breeze at your back to push you along. But ease is not what the Christian life is all about. It is more of a moving into the face of strong resistance caused by cross currents of worldly trends. It has never been the desire of God to have His people pushed along by the world, but rather He desires us to turn the world around with truth and right.

Another lesson I learned was that barking dogs never bite . . . as long as they are barking. When they quit, you had better watch out because they may be doing something else . . . this includes biting. Now I guess there may be any number of analogies from this episode. But the one I would like to emphasize has to do with distractions along life's way. There are many of these to threaten us, and they are a great deal like barking dogs. These diversions draw attention to themselves but generally are not big as problems go. We tend to worry and fret over circumstances that surround us. Some of the worries are real, some imaginary. The basic difficulty is that we get our eyes off of where we should be going and fix our gaze on where we should not be going. This can cause problems and a wandering from the right path. In fact, while we are transfixed by watching a small object we can well be run down by a much larger one. While looking at the small yellow cat we can be hit by a semi-truck. Or put it another way . . . while we are dwelling upon our small worries we could be getting into larger spiritual problems.

There are probably many other little illustrations that we could draw from my ride into the country and the experience of a middle-ager fighting the energy crisis with a bicycle. But I'll just let them go for now and remind myself that many pleasant moments are discovered when we are not really looking for them. Even a "Happy Birthday, Dad" sounds good from the family when you would just as soon forget it all. But I guess it is worth going through another birthday—if you get your first new bike.

My Willie Can Do It!

Maternal pride is one of the great wonders of the world. It overlooks problems and sees a son or daughter. My memory of the evidence of such maternal pride takes me back to a neighbor whose son was on the high school football team. He was limited to the number of times he got onto the playing field—which was none. However, as the season progressed the mother's faithfulness in attendance at the games never wavered. She knew in her heart there would be the time when he would be called by the coach to race onto the field and become the hero. Towards the end of the season the call came loud and clear; his opportunity was NOW. As he raced onto the field his foot caught in the chain of the linesman, and with loss of unmeasurable dignity, he went down—untouched by the enemy. Mom had only one concern—was her Willie hurt?

Mothers are like that, and all of us sons and daughters appreciate this beyond measure. Mothers of other generations were much like mothers of today. Even mothers who are mentioned in the Bible had great faith in their children's ability. Such a humanly touching account is told of the mother of James and John. Their mother was so confident of their abilities she made an astounding request of the Lord. "Let my two boys have a special place in heaven" was the essense of her request. "Grant that these my two sons may sit, the one on thy right hand and the other on the left in thy kingdom" (cf. Matt. 20:20-22). I don't know what the other mothers of the disciples thought about this, but we do know what Jesus thought about it. For He replied, "Ye know not what ye ask." She felt her sons could do whatever needed to be done.

It has been said the true worth of a man rests somewhere between his mother's opinion of him and his mother-in-law's opinion of him. One of the two has the ability to be more objective than the other, and for good cause. I am certain the unobjective outlook of a mother is fully born out of a love for her child. But sometimes there are faults in the efforts of love, and hindrances do arise.

How often have overconcern and misdirected love stood in the way of the will of God. There are parents who refuse to give up their child to the Lord and His work. Perhaps, there might be more missionaries in the fields of the world, if love for God could overreach the love of child. Some have said, "We can't give up our child to go to a strange land among backward people." This is not love. This is selfishness and sin if God truly desires the son or daughter to serve Him abroad. Would there really be a shortage of pastors if parents did not direct their children into more lucrative jobs with greater prestige?

If you want to be really proud of your "Willie" take a lesson from an ancient Hebrew lady who prayed for a child and then "lent" him to the Lord. He became a great man of God, and we read about Samuel and teach our children about Samuel because there was a Hannah. God took this young lad and what an influence for God he became. God is not only looking for Samuels today, He is looking for Hannahs as well.

Share your children with God and God will share them with the needs of a humanity that is lost in the darkness and confusion of this world. Once they are shared and have served for God, He will take care of the honors and the crowns which He gives to His faithful servants.

Nevertheless, with too much dependence on himself and

his own personal abilities, "Willie" may well trip over the chain markers before he gets into the action. But, turn him loose—and watch him make a spiritual contribution for the Lord, and people will call him blessed in appreciation for his spiritual contribution to them.

A Government School for Coyotes

(The sheep are being attacked again)

Some things must be seen to be believed, and even then one is not certain. But let me tell you what I saw and heard, and I will give you the opportunity to accept or reject it. I had settled down to the evening news and everything was just about normal—very gloomy. But the next sequence was different. It was an account of the diminishing sheep herds in the West. It seems the sheep population is not doing well, and one of the menacing problems is caused by the coyotes. Their number is increasing, and they are preying on the poor sheep.

Of course this is a real problem to the sheepherders and they have sought some solutions. The logical one is to shoot the coyotes. But in this day and age there would quickly arise an organization called "Save the Coyotes, Incorporated." This dedicated group would raise a million dollars toward the printing and distribution of literature. Then in a few months all of us would be weeping and crying for the righteous cause of the coyotes. (I think there must already be an organization to save the mosquitoes—they are doing so well!)

So how do you stop the coyote problem and save the sheep? This, friends, is when we appreciate having such an efficient government—one to turn to in time of any need. The government, upon due consideration, proposed a solution to the problem by means of educating the coyotes not to attack sheep. Now, here is a simple answer to the whole matter. It works like this—you catch the coyote and send it to the special government school. The instructors take a white rabbit and put a chemical on it, and when the coyote attacks the prey—the results are obvious. From now on the coyote will leave all *white* animals alone. You run a black rabbit by, and again the coyote attacks. No chemical is on the black rabbit. So you see the mean coyote has been educated. They did not say what degree is given to the graduate of the government school, but I think it is an AOBA, which means Attack Only Black Animals.

But even the government has a couple of problems. The coyotes are notoriously poor school attenders, and the rate of dropouts is unbelievable. There must be the problem of busing the animals as well. The other problem is that, if the graduate has learned his lesson well, there are always *black* sheep in the flock! It looks like the best answer to the whole problem is for the shepherds to spend more time and effort in protecting their sheep.

Being a sheep has never been an easy life. The Bible talks often about the difficulties and the dangers that can come to such defenseless little animals. They need someone to care for them and provide for their needs at all times. If not, they get into big trouble and eventually perish. Jesus compared His earthly children to sheep in John, the tenth chapter, and pointed out how there is not only a need for a shepherd but for a *good* shepherd. There are good ones, and then there are those who do their work just for the gain they obtain from it. Without the right person to watch over and protect them, there are more problems to cope with than the average sheep can overcome.

The Old Testament speaks of Christ as the Lamb for slaughter, and John the Baptist spoke of the Lamb of God. Where there is a lamb there is usually an enemy to threaten its very existence. From the spiritual point of view, the world is literally filled with evil "coyotes." In fact, the name itself has come to mean "a contemptible sneak." So there is no rest for God's lambs in this evil world. That contemptible sneak, Satan, is forever trying to get into the flock and carry away and destroy all he can.

What is the solution for today? Well, the government took the oldest method by seeking to *educate* the problem away. Do not blame this approach too much. Education has been an accepted method for a long time. When you take a sinner and educate him, you only elevate the level of transgressions. For instance, take a simple thief—he steals apples and many small objects. Give him a degree in electronics, and he then can use the computer to help him steal ten million dollars worth of merchandise. You did not change the man, you merely refined his methods.

So it seems the responsibility is now back on the owner of the sheep to care for these needy animals. I am thankful to know that when I gave my life to Jesus Christ I trusted my future, both in time and eternity, to the Good Shepherd who has full power to save and to keep His sheep to the uttermost.

I'm OK, You're OK, But He's Perfect

My Favorite Reflections

Right at the top of the best-seller list week after week is another one of those books on people relationships. This subject is always a good one for book sales because people just are not getting along with each other very well these days. There is also the apparent desire on the part of people to try to understand themselves a little better. So the book *I'm OK—You're OK* tells us how to understand each other and accept ourselves and others. It certainly has caught on with readers and continues to sell at a rapid rate.

I assure you the author does not have all the answers; though much of the material has value. Unfortunately, many individuals run from one new book on personal problems to the other. Following the teachings of this author and then the next becomes a consuming pastime. They end up with a mental whiplash and are in worse condition than when they started.

One of the problems of modern psychology is not the outright rejection of God as much as it is the total absence of reference to God. In seeking to get along with other people (which is what we spend a lot of our time doing), we begin to compare ourselves with those we meet. It finally results in something like this—to avoid hostility, I will accept you, if you will accept me. We mentally shake hands at this point and go about our business. Something like this is necessary because no one is perfect, and we have to adjust to the other fellow—because really he has more problems than I do! (Oh, humility thou art a blessed thing.) While we are accepting each other with all of our problems, I say I'm OK and I guess you're OK—so there is the solution. This may lull us into a feeling of security. If all is well between us mortals—then all is well in the world.

This false security comes from an inaccurate and baseless comparison and evaluation among ourselves.

I'm OK and you're OK, but the problem is —*He is perfect.* He, being God, is actually the One that makes it difficult for us because we must meet His standards. A dog can be large beside an ant; but be small beside a horse. At this stage a horse feels great about his size until he stands beside a giraffe. But alas! the giraffe gets a complex when he meets an elephant. Thus, comparisons are difficult and do not prove anything. You, as a Christian, may "feel good" in your moral status as compared to a person who makes no pretense of seeking to do right. You may even be more than satisfied alongside of a part-time church member. But the true test is how are you doing when you use as a yardstick the One who is perfect—God?

Man, by human wisdom, seeks to make us all "feel better." Somehow the good feeling is so evasive in life. It really comes not so much by seeking for it as it does in knowing and responding. To know the way and the will of God and to follow them brings the peace and satisfaction people are so desperately seeking. To give our lives to Christ in salvation and to follow Him in obedience brings both peace with God and peace with man.

An honest appraisal of the whole situation is—I'm not so OK and You're not so OK. But He is perfect. Hopeless future for mankind? No. Thank God, He wants to begin a work in us that will result in us being *like* Him some day.

Whatever Happened to $1.98 Sneakers?

Inflation is not a new word at all. It has been around for generations. Fifteen years ago we could have given a vague definition if we cared to, but why worry about unimportant subjects . . . that was the domain of the economists. Today things are different because if anyone knows the difference between a nickel and a quarter, he can tell you about the practical implications of inflation. Ask a buyer in any company . . . he will tell you! Ask a housewife and then be prepared for a half-hour discourse on what has happened to her food budget. Inflation is listed as the number one problem for the majority of people these days.

It came home forcibly to me the other day when my son wanted to buy a pair of athletic shoes. When I was young (not too many years ago), we called them sneakers and they cost about $1.98 a pair. But if you want to give them a dignified title—so what? Jeff said he preferred Pro-Keds and that sounded a little classy for tennis shoes—but, again, no problem. I had ten extra dollars and being in a generous mood I thought I might surprise him and get him a blue pair as well as a red pair. Upon arrival at the shoe store, I casually looked around and then concluded that sneakers had come a long way. They were made of leather and looked like something Jerry Lucas would wear. When I looked at the box, the end with the price markings, I felt some mistake must have been made. The price—$26.95.

My protests only met with an unbelievable statement—"These are not the expensive ones, Dad, the good ones cost $35." My "fond" memory of sneakers was never that great, to be truthful. After having worn them all day, my personal desire was to remove them from the room and put them in private isolation where they could continue to regenerate through the night by themselves. Neither their appearance nor fragrance appealed to either my eyes or nose. And now they were $35! It seemed some cruel hoax had been perpetrated on humanity. Was this inflation or a Halloween trick? It was *inflation,* I was soon to discover.

My, how things have changed and the cost of living has gone up at an unbelievable rate! It is difficult at times to adjust my mid-aged mentality to the realities of a world gone wild. After having surrendered to the "cheap"pair and great damage to my credit card, I found myself paying a tax on my purchase just about equal to what I used to pay for the full price on shoes. As I left the store I had one bright bit of hope. My son was wearing Pro-Keds—the same kind of sneakers those guys wear who are seven feet tall and make a million dollars a year dropping a basketball through the top of a peach basket. I never made it with my old sneakers, but maybe he would.

Yet I wonder if anyone is happier than we kids were, even though we did not have so many luxuries. The beauty of being poor when I grew up was that none of us knew we were poor. We did not have a thousand politicians running around giving us "underprivileged" kids help. Our parents worked for what they got and they were too proud to take a handout. All they asked for was an opportunity to be able to work. We were taught respect for all property because it did not come easy, and it was the fruit of someone else's labors.

It is that time of the year again when we come to Thanksgiving. It makes me realize that the possession of so many good things has caused us to only covet more, and we fail to be thankful for what we already have. Plenty, if not accepted with thanksgiving, will only result in greed. Certainly we have more than ever before, yet we complain more than we ever have in the past. Humanity is made up of a strange group of individuals—touched by sin and blinded by desire they have forgotten the Creator and the Giver of all good gifts. It is time to be reminded that God gave, not only His Son, but all precious gifts. In the midst of plenty, it is time to quit greedily grasping for everything in sight. Stop a minute and offer sincere thanks to the Heavenly Father.

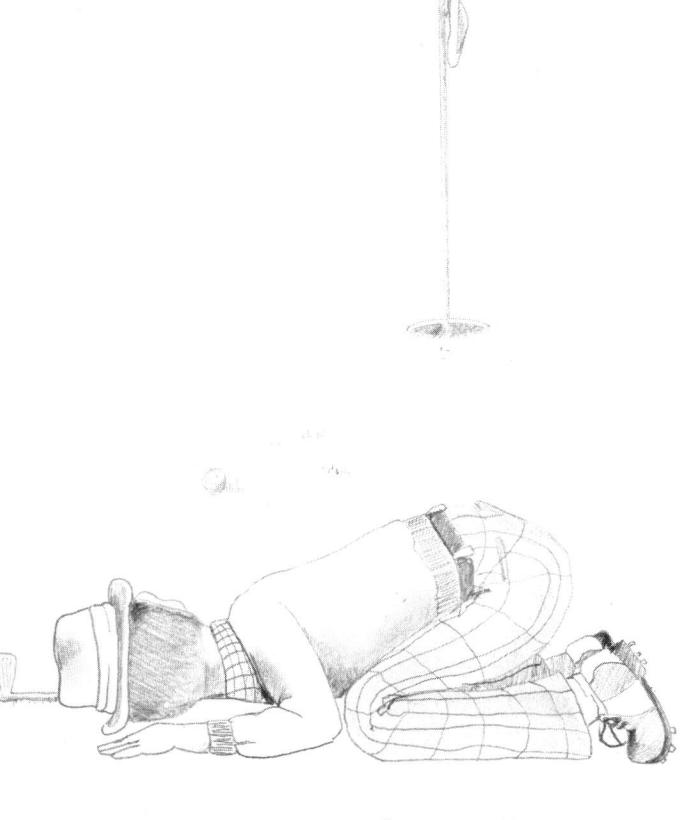

Analysis Paralysis

My Favorite Reflections • 53

Several weeks ago I found myself seated before the TV with a touch of escapism and the real world all shut out. I was watching the closing round of a major golf tournament. Outside my window was the cold winter snows of Indiana, but on my screen was the warm picture of Hawaii. Before me were the best golfers of the world making shots that defied my fondest hopes. What a world to escape to during the woes of winter! I had been hoping my hero, Arnold Palmer, would somehow make the big move in the late rounds. But it was not to be. The Arnie of old has not been making those big moves like he used to do. The young kids on the circuit have been doing very well. Still my heart was hoping for the middle-aged athlete to show those kids.

My interest began to wane, when all of a sudden the announcer said something that really struck me. One of the golfers was on the green and about to putt. He apparently was trying to decide which way the ball would roll towards the hole. Would it go to the right, would it go to the left, maybe straight ahead? To a non-golfer this may sound like a very unimportant problem, but to this golfer it was of paramount importance. First prize money was about $50,000. The longer the golfer looked — the harder was the decision. The announcer said, "I think he has Analysis Paralysis."

I came back to my real world very quickly. What a graphic description of much of our way of life! We are always having meetings with minicommittees, enlarged committees, executive committees, and maxicommittees. We meet with boards till we are bored. We analyze till we are analyzing our analyses. We are really suffering a bad case of analysis paralysis. By the time we decide how to solve a problem, there is a new problem and the old one isn't a problem anymore. Be certain, I am not advocating jumping into a situation without careful prayer and thought. I suggest counting the cost before becoming involved. However, I don't think it is right to use too much prolonged thought about a subject just as an escape for action. Often the security blanket of a committee meeting helps us to delay making the plunge into the icy waters of reality.

After careful discussion and planning a decision must be made. Action is the next necessary step. Once this is started it should require our full resources and energy. The full thrust of our dedication to God and His work now takes over. We are involved at this point.

More good thoughts and intentions have been lost in committee meetings than anywhere else in the world. That committee meeting on the borders of Caanan cost the Israelites forty years of time and a lot of suffering. The analysis paralysis said: "My, oh my, they are big ones! They are giants and we are so small. They make us look and feel like grasshoppers" (author's translation). The committee by its ten-to-two vote, said We can't do it!" The point they missed was that God had said they could and should move into the land.

Charlie Jones makes a telling statement when he says: "Did you ever see a statue in a city park erected to a committee?" I have seen a list of names on a plaque in a park, but I don't remember a single name. However, I do remember the Washington, Lincoln, Jefferson, and Kennedy memorials.

Consider, pray, decide, and then expend your energy to

the glory of God and to the project God assigns you. Certainly haste makes waste, but inactive hesitation results in stagnation, too.

A Nickel Tip and Gospel Tract

Often the customs and the traditions of our times draw circles around our lives like outlines on a football field. We are to walk with caution between the lines and not step over them or we will be out of bounds. Many of these little nuisances are not to our choosing, but in the eyes of the onlooker they become unwritten laws. One of these every-day encounters is to be found at the end of the dining-out session. Whether the waitress has been late in serving, or she has poured a cup of coffee over your freshly cleaned suit matters little—it is tipping time.

I am never quite ready for the politeness that comes toward the end of a meal. Knowing the hour of trial has come for her, the young lady who has neglected you for the past forty minutes now devotes her undivided attention to those critical moments before you leave the table to pay the bill. She warms your coffee and is willing to stir it with her finger if necessary. It is tip time! Being an average American male member of our middle-class society, I reach into my pocket and put the customary tip under the plate. However, it is exposed in direct proportion to the amount. If it is a generous tip, I let it all show. If it is small, I push it under the plate as far as possible. Having done my duty, I race to the cash register feeling either proud or guilty.

I have found that tips do not always reach their destination. My son, when he was very little, would cart them off if I did not watch. It has come to my attention, from various sources, that wives have lingered for a moment and some extra grocery money was theirs. Frequently they get away with this form of thievery for years before an alert waitress hits their knuckles with the blunt side of a knife handle.

Aside from these minor problems, there is another type of tipping for which I have greater disdain. It is the nickel tip and the gospel tract approach. With full knowledge that the following observations could get me into trouble, I proceed without caution. There is nothing wrong with a nickel tip if that is all the waitress deserves. If you want to stand on the table and shout you had rotten service—more power to you. But let's not make this occasion a time for an evangelistic meeting. The distrubution of a gospel tract is to help a person come to know about the love of God and the salvation of Jesus Christ. When you leave a tip that is below the standard of that which is recognized as the norm of the day, you have left a bad image in the mind of the waitress. Whether right or wrong, whether you believe in tipping or abhor it from the depths of your wallet, you have not made a friend. The appearance of a gospel tract at this moment has one reaction and it is a very negative one. In her mind you have said, "I am cheap" and further in her mind she thinks . . . that is the way those church people are. You must admit, gospel tracts are cheaper than putting another quarter or fifty cents on the table. If you leave a good tract leave a good tip.

I wonder how many unsaved business people have been turned off by the attitude of the church and ministers. Talk to unsaved people in a community who do business with ministers and they can tell you stories that will make you blush. Does the average owner of a business owe a clergyman a share of his profits? I think not! However, that is what a discount really is . . . the businessman's profit—right out of his pocket. Show me one place where the world is asked to pay the Christian's way. We can preach our hearts out and then turn our testimony into ashes by our thoughtless actions toward the world. These attitudes are a carry-over from the time when the clergy was paid in potatoes, corn and produce each week. Such ideas should have died out with the advent of the pickle barrel in the local grocery.

Hold your head up, church and pastor, and put your hand in your pocket instead of reaching out to take. We have come to give to the world life and light, not to go around as beggars having the world look down on us. Let's quit asking and start giving! Maybe your banker, or your waitress, or the local furniture man will start listening to you when you start assuming an honest attitude toward the world in which we live.

Rumble Seats, Running Boards, and Patriotism

If the title catches you and you know what I am talking about, I conclude you are either journeying through or have passed middle age. Being a relatively young middle-ager, I must admit to the knowledge of what rumble seats were really like and how a running board had unquestionable merit. (Compare the ease offered by the running board to the physical gymnastics necessary to enter a present-day automobile!) At this stage in history I feel almost compelled to try to identify the word "patriotism" since there is so little of it around these days. Yes, we have a lot of politics but very little patriotism, and there is a big, big difference.

The reason for grouping these three things together is that obviously they all appear to be out of style. However, I think it would not be too bad an idea to have all three return to the American scene. It could be very refreshing.

Some things lose their value with age, while others gain their weight in gold—and then some! There seems to be an epidemic of seeking old objects—we call it collecting antiques. When an article gets to be over twenty years old in the United States we label it an antique. In Europe when something becomes two hundred years old, it gains the title of "antique."

I must admit to being a skeptic about this antique collecting. I am tempted to view it as the distribution of junk by the smart and "bargain buying" by the otherwise. Each one smiles at his transaction and thinks he has really been wise. As long as they are both happy, I guess all is well. When I visit an antique shop I weep for my parents. They might be wealthy if they had not thrown out all those items we had in the house during the depression days of the 1930's. Campaign buttons we had; Boker Coffee Banks —a plenty; a Mickey Mouse watch—certainly; Shirley Temple doll—naturally; even insulators from the telephone lines. If we had only held out long enough to share in the great antique sales of the seventies!

While we collect the junk of two generations ago, we discard the values taught and held to be self-evident by these same generations. Some of the old ideas are being cast aside as bad and not up to date for an enlightened people. Values of the home are being changed—can you remember when it was a real disgrace to have a divorce in the family? I heard recently of a reception being held for a woman on the occasion of her divorce. Her friends came and brought her gifts. There are many other former values that have been changed with the passing of years, and one is the attitude towards our nation. We call it patriotism.

In recent years the war in Vietnam brought a noticable change of attitude in our country. It raised doubts in the minds of young people as to where their loyalties really rested. The rapidly rising concept of "do your own thing" and enjoy yourself—was with us. The young people rebelled on campuses and burned the flag. There was an open defiance of the country and the establishment—the very people that happened to be feeding and clothing and providing for the rebelling ones. They sang a song, "Where Have All the Young Men Gone?" I have contended that the young men have not gone anywhere. They are still here. But they are much harder to recognize.

On top of the defiance of many came the present disillusionment with politics and political leaders. This has been followed by a distrust of the press, and the church, and other established organizations. So patriotism is at a very low level in this country today, and the same or similar conditions can be seen throughout the world. What an opportunity for a new world leader!

Yet, those who would condemn and tear down have not offered us anything to replace their destruction. Certainly, there is a lot wrong today. But let's not throw the baby out with the bath water. I, as a Christian, can still be thankful for the freedom, though it may be diminishing, which permits me to worship and serve God.

As I have stated before, I still get a chill from watching the flag being run up the pole. I love to sing "America" and "The Star Spangled Banner" still touches me. (My friends wish I could sing it in key and on pitch though!) My loyalty to God rates first in priority, but loyalty to the principles of my country ranks high. Call it nostalgia if you wish, but I still thank God He permitted me to be born an American.

A Stone, Some Paint, and Thanks

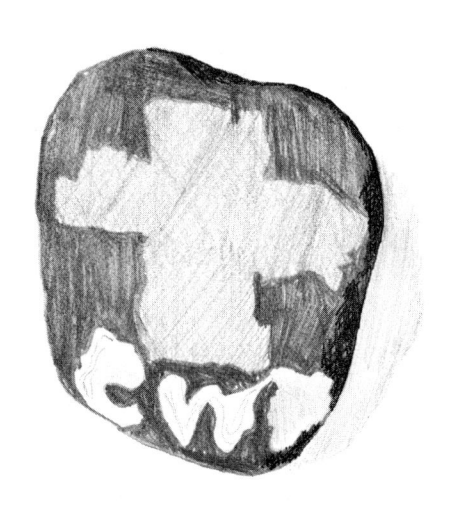

Thanksgiving comes through to the average American as a patriotic and religious holiday—with a lot of good eating thrown in as a bonus. The sermons we hear or deliver are somewhat stilted and repetitious. It all turns out as a difficult time to express our innermost thoughts in terms to be really understood. We feel it, but saying it is a little frustrating.

Let me try to express my thoughts somewhat different this year. I have on my desk a paperweight. It has been with me for a number of years. As far as paperweights go it certainly leaves a lot to be desired. Let me try to describe it for you. It is a stone covered with dark blue paint. On this stone is painted a green cross and below the cross in yellow letters appear the initials C.W. and another letter that is very, very blurry and appears to be just another dab of yellow paint. But though it is not clear, I know very well the dab or blob of paint is a T. Now, wait a minute before you ask the question—What did you pay for something like that? I'll admit it looks like I was taken by a poor workman with a fast tongue. However, it didn't cost me a penny. It was a gift.

The giver was a young boy who did the best he could on a project at his school. He was very young when he did the work, which probably shows clearly in the workmanship on the finished product. But one day this young boy proudly brought his completed masterpiece to me and said: "Here is something for you. Thanks, Dad." The "thanks" is remembered and the small blue stone has been on my desk for several years. I rather imagine it will stay there for many more years, and the only one who I would ever think of giving it to would be the one who made it for his dad.

Saying thanks . . . children to their Heavenly Father . . . is what Thanksgiving is all about. It is God's redeemed children taking a special day for remembering all of His provisions for us. "He giveth to all life, and breath, and all things" (Acts 17:25). He is the supplier of all the good things we have and all of the good things we yet hope by faith to obtain. Thus, all thanks belong to Him.

It makes us wonder oftentimes what really pleases God. We know from the Scriptures what we ought to do in acts of obedience. Worship, service and obedience are necessary parts of our Christian lives. Yet, I think we often miss the obvious in our search for truth. I really surmise God wants our complete beings—our thoughts, words and deeds. It could be that the acts we think to be of relative unimportance just might be near the top of the list of God's desires. We might try to bring to Him some tokens of our love with the words: "Thank you, Father, for all You have done." Not that we can give God anything He really needs, for He is certainly self-sufficient. Nevertheless, He looks for the expressions of our love.

Could it be your thankfulness would be best expressed by spending some time alone with God? Take the time to say you love Him very much. Replace some moments with your friends, with a few minutes with Him. I know it all sounds like a stone or rock, painted with a rather uneven coat of blue paint, but there is a cross painted on it with your name inscribed. You could thank him, and perhaps your feeble words would be a treasure to the great God of this universe.

This type of prayer and praise would make Thanksgiving

Day a great deal better for you, and the true value could well be reflected through you to others. It would above all things make Thanksgiving what it really is—A Time of Thanks.

You Can't Hit a Home Run Every Time

This summer I have had an opportunity to see the Cubs, Tigers, and Orioles—without going by the zoo. The Giants and the Reds were also there, without benefit of a trip to a circus or to China. Yes, it was at the "old ball park." My interest in baseball has been on the downgrade for some years, this due mainly to the fact that I spent most of my days somewhere in the Northern Ohio area. This placed me close to Cleveland. And the way the Indians have been playing for the past few years, and being a person who shrinks from suffering, I just about abandoned all interest. But, being the father of a twelve-year-old boy has helped spark some new interest in this pastime.

So I have seen a few games this year at Chicago, Cincinnati and Detroit. I was a little surprised to hear boos for one of the local heroes at a recent game. It seems that he was in a slump; had not been performing too well in the field. Above all, his hitting was very bad. As he came to the plate, abusive words and sounds were heard from the stands. By the sound of things you would think that he had been stealing ice cream from all of the local children, or had committed some equally villainous act. He stepped into a fast ball and in the words of the bleacher fans he really "parked one"—a home run. To see the change in the crowd was absolutely amazing—they stood and cheered! For the balance of the evening his every act met with full approval of the 48,000 fans. I thought to myself—it certainly would be nice if you could hit a home run every time.

But that is impossible to do. There never has been a ball player that ever accomplished it. In fact, when it comes to hits, if you can get just 3 out of 10 that makes you a 300 hitter! And if you haven't heard yet, that is a select category for a ball player. That evening, far from the shouts of the crowd, I began to think of the spiritual application of it all. The imperfection of the batter and reaction of the crowd brought to mind the plight of Christian workers and the judgments of their observers. The actions and reactions in the arena of Christian service bring boos of criticism and the cheers of approval.

In Christian service *no one* hits a home run every time. "No one" includes the pastor, Sunday School superintendent, deacon, teacher, usher, and even the janitor (he misses a cobweb now and then). Each Christian who truly has the work of God as his goal "strikes out" more often than he wants. It is not that he wants to strike out, but when you are in there trying there is the ever-present possibility of failure. The one who does not try may think he is avoiding failure, but he has already failed because he did not try.

It is disappointing to put forth an effort such as preaching a sermon, teaching a class, or visiting an unchurched person; and then to have the feeling that it just didn't turn out right. At least the immediate result was not what you had prayed for. But remember, you had the right motive. And perhaps future results could be more positive than they first appeared.

Then there is the crowd in the stand, the onlookers. They are the ones who watch, but do not participate. Their main talent is the ability to be vocal—and vocal they are! Each move of the pastor or other Christian worker receives their close attention. After observation they will cast their approval or disapproval, their vocal analysis of the action. But the action that really counts is that of the "player," and whether by the help of God he did his best in service for the Lord. He may at times hear the jeers from the crowd, but his goal is to hear a well done from the Lord. The crowd's attitude can be fickle—changing from boos to blessing—but the one to please is God. "Therefore, my beloved brethren, be ye stedfast, unmoveable, always abounding in the work of the Lord, forasmuch as ye know that your labour is not in vain in the Lord" (I Cor. 15:58).

A Progressive Alternative to Busing

One of the secrets of success is to be a step ahead of someone else. This is not always an easy task to accomplish because the active mind can come up with some mighty clever and innovative ideas. In this day and age the church is not in an isolated world of its own, but it is continually affected by progressive ideas of promotion. I do not intend to infer that all these so-called modern "Madison Avenue" ideas are either right or wrong. The goal of using a variety of means to bring people under the hearing of the gospel of Jesus Christ might well be justified by using the statement of Paul that all means and methods are in order. I stand amazed at the original concepts of promotion that separate the men from the boys when it comes to attracting people.

Let me cite a few of some of the working ideas that stand out like stellar stars in attracting people. In the "Olden Days" there was a very simple little gimmick called the Record-Breaking Sunday. On the momentous day when the attendance in Sunday School passed the previous goal, someone shattered a shiny black record of "Heavenly Sunshine." Since our method of recording has changed, the modern version of this event is to unravel a cassette and call it Pull-Out-the-Tape Sunday. We occasionally have a Pack-a-Pew Sunday, but that is almost "old hat" now. Promising snow on Christmas Day is an effective promotion deal—particularly if you are in a climate where the temperature will be in the 90s (more or less). A California pastor was able to deliver this miracle by the use of a snow-making machine.

How about the "World's Largest Sundae"? It helps to use those everpopular "world" phrases, you know. I heard of one pastor who used several hundred gallons of ice cream to pull off the sundae promotion idea. How about the largest popcorn ball? Too late, it has already been discovered. One church recently took everyone to lunch at McDonalds—all 900 of them! If this catches on, McDonalds will keep moving towards the good old 20 billion mark.

There are other ideas to get people into church, but none has worked as well as the idea of busing. It is a very old idea. As proof of this statement I must admit that as a child I remember seeing Sunday School buses. Before I was very old my father had used several old Fords to transport children of the neighborhood to the First Brethren Church in Akron, Ohio. Later the church purchased a bus, and there is still evidence of the fruit of labor from such efforts. People were brought to church and they found Christ through the teaching of the Word of God.

But simple busing has progressed to a sizable project, and bus fleets have grown as have the churches and Sunday Schools that have used them. I hear of bus routes that extend for hundreds of miles—and this is no joke! Some drivers are scheduled to begin their pick ups at six o'clock in the morning in order to reach the outer limits of their routes. It has been estimated that in completing their rounds some buses may pass as many as a hundred other churches. I would be the last to condemn such zeal because there is so little honest effort exercised to reach out to the millions beyond.

Nevertheless, for the past months I have had a feeling that busing is beginning to probe the outer limits of its potential. What I am saying is—there has to be a better idea —a more up-to-date system. Since someone is sure to think of it sooner or later, let me go on record as the one to suggest the untapped possibility of airlifting. It would break down the limits of those 150-mile bus routes and could reach across state lines. Formerly a church was a neighborhood concept. However, busing has made the church a multicommunity concept, but now airlifting could make it a multistate affair. Think of the same time spent on a bus route being transformed to a plane route. Who will be the first to use a 747 to airlift 300 people from St. Louis to Los Angeles? After all, the time is no problem—we have proved it is not a noticeable handicap. Some pastor in Florida could bring in a load from Memphis, Tennessee, or Atlanta, Georgia, in a little over an hour. He could feed them after the service at McDonalds and have them back home in time to see the Sunday afternoon football game or, better yet, have a TV on the plane!

Does this sound far out to you? For all I know someone has already thought of the idea and is presently selling church bonds to finance the deal. The church is never stagnant in its progress, but just remember you heard it here first—or did you?

Now some of you are scratching your heads and saying, "No, I don't believe it could happen!" It will. The place of progressive ideas in the church is firmly established and buses may someday be as old-fashioned as "record-breaking day." Perhaps in our generation every progressive church may have its own airport. My only hope is the gospel of Jesus Christ will be used to greet each new arrival.

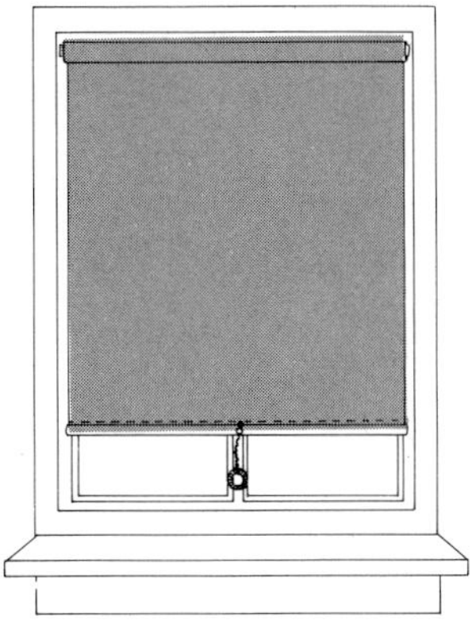